Leading
HAPPINESS

by Travis Hellstrom

LEADING HAPPINESS

LEADERSHIP AND HAPPINESS AT WORK IN CERTIFIED B CORPORATIONS

A Qualitative Study of Leaders and Employees To Understand The Influence of Shared

Leadership on Worker Happiness within Certified Benefit Corporations

Travis Hellstrom

PIM72

A Capstone Paper submitted in partial fulfillment of the requirements

for a Masters of Arts in Service, Leadership and Management Development

at SIT Graduate Institute in Brattleboro, Vermont.

July 25TH, 2014

Advisor: Dr. Aqeel Tirmizi, Ph.D.

ACKNOWLEDGEMENTS

I have a lot of special people to thank. First, I would like to thank my advisor and mentor Aqeel Tirmizi. Your mentorship, patience and faith in me during my time at SIT Graduate Institute has been simply incredible. Thank you for being such a great teacher and friend. SIT is very lucky to have you.

Thank you Amy for your support and humor throughout this entire process. Your friendship is priceless and I look forward to trying to pay you back. Thank you Judy for your kind feedback on my writing and helping me stay grounded. Thank you Ashley for your advice and support. Thank you Alex, Jeannie, Marlee, Bonnie, Gerry, Yvonne, Alana, Carolina, Christopher, Ian, Steve, David, Asma, Keiko, Todd, Chiara, Dede, Darren and John for being great friends and classmates.

Thank you to my family for your love and encouragement. Thank you Tunga for your unconditional support during long nights and long days full of classes and responsibilities. I loved being able to come home to you every night, especially after those 10^{PM} classes. Thank you Mom, Dad, Anna, Eli, Jill, Bryan, Merih, Michael and Seang for your love and a great summer that helped me relax and focus. Thank you Big Nanny for believing in me and always saying "That sounds wonderful" every time I told you what I was doing at school.

Thank you also Casey, John, Brian, Evan, Kelsie and the en*theos team for your love and support in my final thesis months. I'm honored to be helping you become the newest greatest Certified B Corps in the world.

Thank you to Bart, Jay and Andy for leading this special movement and Charity, Jessica, Kate, Duane, Mende, Batzaya, Boldkhuu and Uyanga for sharing your stories with me.

DEDICATION

I would like to dedicate this thesis to Big Nanny and Papa Jack,

my grandmother and grandfather.

I really wish you could have been here to read it with me.

Thank you for inspiring me to use my talents to change the world.

Thank you for showing me that it's what I do with what I have that matters.

Thank you for helping me see that being an adult is a choice.

Thank you for being a beacon of love and inspiration in my life.

Thank you for being who you were.

Thank you for helping me become who I am today.

"The very purpose of life is happiness, the very notion of our life is towards happiness." *The Dalai Lama*

CONSENT TO USE STATEMENT

I hereby grant permission for World Learning to publish my capstone on its website and in any of its digital/electronic collections, and to reproduce and transmit my Capstone electronically. I understand that World Learning's websites and digital collections are publicly available via the Internet. I agree that World Learning is not responsible for any unauthorized use of my capstone by any third party who might access it on the Internet or otherwise.

Student Signature:

June 25TH, 2014

TABLE OF CONTENTS

ABSTRACT

The Certified B Corps movement is setting a new standard for businesses, committing to a multiple stakeholder orientation focused on community, environment and the workplace in addition to financial profit. More than 1,000 companies, including well-known companies like Patagonia, Ben & Jerry's, King Arthur Flour, and Etsy, have joined the ranks of Certified B Corps in over 30 countries.

The B Corps certification is understood to promote a set of organizational practices, which envision improved employee performance and well-being. An important element of that well-being is employee happiness. Previous research has shown that improved business leadership practices can have significant impact on happiness in the workplace, which in turn can show measurable gains in productivity, sales, and overall workplace performance. However, no studies have been done on unique practices present within Certified B Corporations and the unique workplaces B Corps leaders are creating. This research focuses on how two successful startup Certified B Corps are influencing happiness in their workplaces through unique leadership strategies, from the perspectives of both the leaders and the employees within those companies.

The current study examined leadership practices and their impact on employee performance and happiness in two B Certified organizations. The results showed that shared leadership practices are not only pervasive at all levels in both companies; they are creating positive workplace environments that are unprecedented in the lives of those involved. This has important implications for the future of the B Corps movement and the changing world of business and merits further research.

Keywords: Benefit Corporations, Happiness at Work, Startups, Shared Leadership, Management

INTRODUCTION

I came to business and benefit corporations by way of the Peace Corps and a personal mission to help others. I have always believed in helping others which drew me to work in the medical field initially through high school and college, but after my studies in college I was drawn more to Peace Corps than to medical school. After three years of service in Mongolia I was introduced to the benefit corporation movement by a friend and mentor who I worked with to create the first TEDx event in Mongolia. I became part of his startup company, focused my work on philanthropy, and entered graduate school focused on how to better understand making business a force for good in the world. Unlike the doctor's office, which we visit when we are sick, the office is a place people find themselves almost every day of the week for decades of their lives. I think this makes business a huge potential for good in the world.

Over the past two years I have worked closely with multiple Certified Benefit Corporations and been struck by their commitment to their stakeholders in the community, their dedication to the environment and their focus on workplace happiness in addition to financial profit. When I began graduate school the Certified B Corporation movement was just over 400 companies strong and B Corps could be found in only half a dozen countries. A year and a half later not only have increasingly well-known companies like Patagonia joined the ranks of Certified B Corps, but now more than 1,000 companies are certified in over 30 countries. The movement is growing faster every day and, as Esquire Magazine wrote recently, "B Corps might turn out to be like civil rights for blacks or voting rights for women - eccentric, unpopular ideas that took hold and changed the world."

One thing that draws all Certified Benefit Corporations together is a requirement to measure key performance indicators in a public assessment available to anyone. The areas measured fall under four main categories Governance, Workers, Community and Environment. With this publicly available data using indicators that are easy to understand it becomes possible to measure outcomes like happiness at work. The Worker sections of the survey, for instance, assesses each company's relationship to its workforce: how the company treats its workers through compensation, benefits, training, ownership opportunities, work environment, management communication, job flexibility, corporate culture, and worker health and safety. This data is particularly valuable and interesting not only to companies but also academics and organizational leaders. In organizations with high scores in the worker happiness, what is being done differently and what role does shared leadership play?

Whether you look back at our constitution which founded a country on the idea of the pursuit of happiness as an inalienable right of all people, read the words of ancient philosophers like Aristotle who said, "Happiness is the meaning and the purpose of life, the whole aim and end of human existence" or more modern philosophers and Nobel Peace Prize winners like The Dalai Lama who said, "The very purpose of life is happiness, the very notion of our life is towards happiness," happiness is a pillar of human life. It is also an important business matter. In a recent meta-analysis of happiness research which brought together over 200 scientific studies on nearly 275,000 people, they found that "happiness leads to success in nearly every domain of our lives, including marriage, health, friendship, community involvement, creativity, and, in particular, our jobs, careers, and businesses" (Lyubomirsky, King, & Diener, 2005). "The list of the benefits of happiness in the workplace goes on and on," writes Shawn Achor in The Happiness Advantage, "Data abounds showing that happy workers have higher levels of productivity, produce higher sales, perform better in leadership positions, and receive higher performance ratings and higher pay. They also enjoy more job security and are less likely to take sick days, to quit, or to become burned out. Happy CEOs are more likely to lead teams of employees who are both happy and healthy, and who find their work climate conducive to high performance" (2010, p. 70).

Shared leadership is a relatively new area of academic interest, but it has several holes. According to scholars Carson, Peace and Conger, some of the major areas in shared leadership that need more research are events that generate shared leadership, facilitation factors, life cycles in shared leadership settings and outcomes of shared leadership (Carson et al., 2007; Pearce and Conger, 2002). This research, including Certified Benefit Corporation assessments and informational interviews can begin to fill these holes. In this research I examined if qualities defining shared leadership can be identified as being practiced in Certified B Corporations and if that leadership is influencing greater happiness at work. If shared leadership is an accessible way for supervisors to be better leaders and influence workplace happiness, it would have clear implications for all leaders who want to increase productivity and happiness in their organizations. Specifically I sought to answer how shared leadership influences worker happiness within Certified Benefit Corporations by looking at the key characteristics of shared leadership, how the B Corporation movement measures worker happiness, what the dimensions of worker happiness are that have been researched and how these characteristics and dimensions appear to be manifesting in Certified B Corporation work environments.

The B Corporation Movement

The Certified B Corporation movement began in 2008 when its founders were convinced there should be a way to encourage and protect corporations who want to make the triple bottom line (people, planet and profit) part of their constitution. According to B Lab, the nonprofit organization behind the B Corporation movement, "B Corp is to business what Fair Trade certification is to coffee or USDA Organic certification is to milk. B Corps are certified by the nonprofit B Lab to meet rigorous standards of social and environmental performance, accountability, and transparency. Today, there is a growing community of more than 1,000 Certified B Corps from 33 countries and over 60 industries working together toward 1 unifying goal: to redefine success in business" (B Lab, 2014).

Traditionally a corporation is beholden to its shareholders and increasing profits in every decision that it makes is a legal requirement. Often this can happen at the expense of the environment, our communities and the workforce. As B Lab writes, "We envision a new sector of the economy which harnesses the power of private enterprise to create public benefit. This sector is comprised of a new type of corporation - the B Corporation - which is purpose-driven, and creates benefit for all stakeholders, not just shareholders."

They go further to define what they call their Declaration of Interdependence, which you can also see in Appendix D. It is written as follows:

"As members of this emerging sector and as entrepreneurs and investors in B

Corporations, We hold these truths to be self-evident:

That we must be the change we seek in the world.

That all business ought to be conducted as if people and place mattered.

That, through their products, practices, and profits, businesses should aspire to do

no harm and benefit all.

To do so, requires that we act with the understanding that we are each dependent upon

another and thus responsible for each other and future generations" (B Lab, 2014).

Through this, B Lab states that, "B Corps and supporters of the movement are redefining success in business and helping build a more inclusive, resilient and sustainable economy. As a result, individuals have greater economic opportunity, society moves closer to achieving a positive environmental footprint, more people are employed in great places to work, and we have built stronger communities at home and across the world."

Currently one of the biggest ways the B Corps movement is making that change is through The B Impact Assessment (BIA). This assessment is currently the most commonly used tool to assess a company's overall social and environmental performance ("B Impact Assessment 101," 2014). It measures the impact of a business on all stakeholders including workers, suppliers, customers, community, and environment. Businesses use the B Impact Assessment to:

- Assess the company's current impact on all stakeholders as measured through 150 easy to answer, educational questions.

- Review and compare their company's B Impact Report, which provides an objective rating of the company's current performance, together with benchmarking information so companies can compare their impact to the impact of thousands of other businesses.

- Improve their impact through access to 30 tools and Best Practice Guides that help in prioritizing and implementing new impact initiatives.   ("B Assessment 101," 2014)

The B Impact Assessment is positive-impact focused, comprehensive, easy to use, educational, transparent, independently governed by the Standards Advisory Councils and is revised at least once every two years (it is currently in version 4). Businesses that use the assessment as a self-assessment tool, including the 15,000 that have used it to date, are self-reporting their information and it is unverified.

However, if a company seeks to become a Certified B Corporation by scoring over an 80 on the assessment, B Lab follows up the assessment with a verification process. This includes an assessment review, supporting documentation, and random on-site reviews. In the assessment review a B Lab staff member sits down with every company seeking certification and spends 60-90 minutes reviewing questions, refining answers and understanding more about the company. During the assessment review the B Lab staff will ask for supporting documentation, and randomly select 8-12 questions that were answered in the affirmative and ask the company to demonstrate those practices in more detail through documentation. Lastly 10% of Certified B Corporations are randomly selected each year for an on-site review with the goal of the review being to verify the accuracy of all affirmative responses in the company's B Impact Assessment. An on-site review typically takes between 6-10 hours depending on the size and scope of business. In order to maintain B Corporation Certification, a company must complete the assessment every two years and achieve at least 80 points. As indicated above,the B Impact Assessment is updated every two years, so recertification also gives companies the opportunity to set improvement goals against the most-up-to-date standard and benchmark their performance over time ("Performance requirements," 2014).

As mentioned before, the assessment measures indicators that fall into four categories: governance, workers, community and environment. For my research I am focusing on workers section and specifically indicators that influence happiness at work. The workers section of the survey assesses each company's relationship to its workforce through 10 areas: how the company treats its workers through compensation, benefits, training, ownership opportunities, work environment, management communication, job flexibility, corporate culture, and worker health and safety. For more details on the assessment you can see Appendix B.

Right now our communities are facing unprecedented challenges around the world - one strategy to meet these challenges is rethinking leadership strategies. This research seeks to understand how shared leadership principles are being used in successful organizations to improve worker happiness. In this research I decided to take measurements already being done through publicly available Certified Benefit Corporation assessments and match them with in-person interviews to highlight the impact of shared leadership principles on workplace happiness. This study adds valuable insight into this important area at a time when our communities need it most.

In addition to the research proposed, I hoped to gain a deeper understanding of inquiry and assessment techniques. More specifically, the personal learning objectives I wished to achieve were to deepen my knowledge of leadership, the benefit corporation movement and effective management skills especially pertaining to how leaders support each other, manage social change together, and stay dedicated to their work through the myriad modern day challenges they face. I also hoped to develop professionally and better articulate my own preferred leadership style, understand the difference between leading and managing, and better understand and discuss issues, theories, and challenges of management and leadership from international to local levels.

LITERATURE REVIEW

The literature review for the proposed research topic will consist of a few major focus areas, including context for shared leadership in the field of leadership study, various research definitions of shared leadership, the effects of shared leadership, key characteristics and measurement of shared leadership, current definitions of happiness at work, major dimensions of worker happiness, and opportunities for further research.

Leadership Field Context

Although leadership has been studied for decades, shared leadership is a relatively new focus of study in the leadership field, with a large number of studies having been done only in the past ten years. I was particularly interested shared leadership since it seemed to describe the unique characteristics I was witnessing in organizations that I admired. While many of them displayed characteristics common in charismatic, transformational and servant leadership, the unique democratic nature of workplaces I was witnessing and horizontal team and organizational structures these companies were using seemed special. It appeared that shared leadership better described these qualities and, with this in mind, I began exploring the concept in more depth.

Before diving into the definitions and effects of shared leadership, it's important to first review leadership studies in a broad sense and then focus in on shared leadership specifically. Several researchers (Bolden, 2004; Williams, Williams, 2008; Hersey & Blanchard, 1988; Horner, 1997), upon reviewing studies throughout the 20th century, concluded that these studies viewed the phenomenon of leadership as attributional, situational and contextual.

Attributional: leadership can be understood through the personal behaviors and characteristics held by the leader. There are several approaches to understanding this, including trait theories that focus on cognitive capacities, personality, social capabilities, and problem-solving skills as well as theories on transactional, transformational and servant leadership (Williams, 2008, p. 149-151).

Situational: leadership can also be understood as a relationship between leaders and followers that varies based on how supportive or directive the leader needs to be. These include the dimensions of supporting, coaching, delegating and directing (Hersey & Blanchard, 1988).

Contextual: leadership can be understood as matching the context in which it occurs. This includes situational leadership as well as action-centered leadership and shared leadership. All of these approaches assume that leadership is understandable and seek to highlight the factors that underlie effective leadership. By better understanding leadership, the modernist approach hopes to help create better leaders and organizations (Williams, 2008, p. 151).

There is also the post-modernist approach which posits that the idea of leadership is a myth, "perpetuat(ing) the idea of leadership to establish an organizing principle which maintains power imbalances in work organizations and other social systems" (Bolden & Kirk, 2006). This critical view asserts that any attempt to understand the truth about leadership, "is like hunting for the Abominable Snowman, or the Holy Grail – a quest that is doomed to failure" (Bolden & Kirk, 2006). The idea here is that leadership is a construct created to perpetuate certain people's self-interest, namely leaders in power, academics, and practitioners, who desire for the field to exist. For example Alvesson and Sveningsson (2003), would argue that "thinking about leadership needs to take seriously the possibility of the non-existence of leadership as a distinct phenomena" (p.359).

The social constructionist view on leadership notes that, regardless of whether it actually exists or not, how people think about leadership matters. In this view leadership is a social construction which, according to Bolden & Kirk (2006):

...neither accepts nor rejects the existence of "leadership" but simply reminds us that the majority, if not all, of what leadership is or appears to be is a subjective construction. Leaders and followers (and others) construct the circumstances that enable the recognition of "leadership" and hence its utility within the social system.

In this way, leadership can be understood as something we do and invent as we go along, not something ready-made or discovered.

All three perspectives inform this proposal and are important to understand shared leadership. Although shared leadership is usually understood through the modernist lens, it's interesting to note that shared leadership presents a challenge for the post-modernist view. As you will see, shared leadership does not seek to "maintain power imbalances in work organizations and other social systems" but voluntarily gives away control to empower all team members.

Definitions of Shared Leadership

Generally speaking, shared leadership is leadership that has been broadly distributed in a team or organization. It is most commonly contrasted with vertical or hierarchical leadership, the dominant leadership model used in most organizations (Bolden, 2011). Other definitions of shared leadership in recent literature include "leadership that emanates from members of teams, and not simply from the appointed leader" (Pearce & Sims, 2001), "a dynamic, interactive influence process among individuals and groups for which the objective is to lead one another to the achievement of group or organizational goals or both" (Pearce & Conger, 2002), and "when two or more members engage in the leadership of the team in an effort to influence and direct fellow members to maximize team effectiveness" (Bergman, Rentsch, Small, Davenport, and Bergman, 2012).

Each of these definitions point to one similarity: shared influence. As Pearce, Manz and Sims write, all definitions of shared leadership include that it is "built upon more than just downward influence on subordinates or followers by an appointed or elected leader. [Shared leadership includes] broadly sharing power and influence among a set of individuals rather than centralizing it in the hands of a single individual who acts in the clear role of a dominant superior" (2009). In *Effective Multicultural Teams*, Ken Williams (2008) writes:

> Traditionally, approaches to leadership focused on individual leaders and concentrated on vertical or hierarchical approaches to organizing work tasks, where followers depend on a leader to direct activities and guide them in implementing decisions in which they were not involved. Shared leadership is the antithesis of this approach, focusing on leadership as a team-level phenomenon (Pearce & Conger, 2003). An ultimate aim of shared leadership is to get team members to share leadership functions, with no one person being designated as the leader and with decisions being made through consensus (Levi, 2001). In order to get to this ultimate aim, teams may begin with a designated leader but then move towards a team structure where there is no designated leader but the leadership functions are shared, or they may decide to rotate leadership so that no one person retains the title of leader. (Williams, 2008, p.154)

Effects of Shared Leadership

Many studies have demonstrated a positive relationship between shared leadership and team effectiveness and performance (Avolio, 2002). Studies have also found it to be a significant predictor of team effectiveness and performance, and often a better predictor than vertical leadership. (Pearce and Sims, 2002; Pearce et al, 2004; Ensley, Hmieleski, & Pearce, 2006).

In a more qualitative study in Forces for Good: The Six Practices of High-Impact Nonprofits, Leslie R. Crutchfield and Heather Grant named shared leadership as one of the most important practices demonstrated by the twelve outstanding nonprofits that they profiled:

The twelve high-impact nonprofits that we studied all had one critical quality in common: they share power and leadership in their quest to be a greater force for good. Despite their individual differences, these leaders have all demonstrated a willingness to distribute leadership among others both inside and outside the organization. Although they may not have started out this way, they all recognized that they cannot increase their impact by hoarding power. The only way to get the top in the social sector is to give power away (Crutchfield & Grant, 2012, pg. 183).

Not surprisingly, shared leadership has been shown to increase the number of leaders and different types of leadership in a group including transformational, transactional and initiating leadership (Bergman et al, 2012; Pearce and Sims, 2002). Shared leadership enables team members to utilize their different abilities and encourages leaders to participate more in the team's decision making and team activities. In the study by Bergman, Rentsch, Small, Davenport, & Bergman (2012), it was also found that each leader only effectively engaged in one type of leadership, leading us to further believe that shared leadership allows for more leadership behaviors to be expressed than vertical leadership.

As shared leadership relates specifically to job satisfaction and happiness at work, Bligh, Pearce and Kohles write in *The importance of self- and shared leadership in team based knowledge work* that, "The development of the self-leadership capabilities of team members sets into motion the meso-level processes that result in higher collective-levels of trust, potency, and commitment, which in turn facilitate the sustained sharing of mutual influence within the team that comprises shared leadership... These assertions are further bolstered by previous research that suggests the increase in duties, responsibility, autonomy and authority associated with self-leadership and shared leadership are linked to other positive team outcomes such as intrinsic motivation (Deci et al., 1989), job satisfaction (Lawler, 1982) and increased effort (Manz, 1992)" (Bligh, Pearce & Kohles, 2006).

Key Characteristics of Shared Leadership

While these definitions and effects are helpful, and even inspirational, the next challenge became moving beyond definitions and identifying key characteristics and ways to measure shared leadership. How do we know shared leadership when we see it. What kinds of questions can we ask in this research that allows us to point and say yes, that is shared leadership.

After researching more deeply in the above research as well as some other resources (Lambert, 2002; Carson, 2007; Porter-O'Grady, 1997; Bligh, 2006), I was able to synthesize five key observable characteristics of shared leadership, Shared Vision & Values, Trust & Openness, Accountability, Interdependence and Ownership, which I describe in detail here.

1. *Shared Vision & Values* - All researchers mentioned this. A shared vision within the shared leadership organization is key (Coluccio & Havlick, 1998). Shared purpose prevails when team members have similar understandings of their team's main objectives and take steps to

ensure a focus on collective goals (Carson, 2007). Shared vision results in coherences. Members reflection on their core values and weave those values into a shared vision to which all can commit themselves. All members of the community continually ask, "How does this practice connect to our vision?" (Lambert, 2002). The core values should be the driving forces underlying the conditions that promote shared leadership, and the mindset behind all of the conditions (Williams, 2008).

2. *Trust & Openness* - At the heart of shared leadership is an overarching mindset or ideology that relies on non-coercion, that is open to learning, that is relationship-oriented, and that is based on building trust (Williams, 2008). A mutually respectful, trusting relationship between individuals who share a common goal based on honest communication (Porter, 1997). Reflective practice consistently leads to innovation. Reflection enables participants to consider and reconsider how they do things, which leads to new and better ways. Participants reflect through coaching, dialogue, and networking (Lambert, 2002). Further, Stephen Covey writes in *The 7 Habits of Highly Effective People,* "Compelling trust is the highest form of human motivation," and quotes Peter Drucker as saying, "Organizations are no longer built on force, but on trust" (Covey, 2013).

3. *Accountability* - Owning the consequences for actions that are inherent in one's role, internally defined, cannot be delegated (Jackson, 2000). Roles and actions reflect broad involvement, collaboration, and collective responsibility. Team members engage in collaborative work, reflection, dialogue, and inquiry that creates the sense that "I share responsibility for learning within our organization" (Lambert, 2002). It is not a democracy; it is an accountability-based approach to structure, in which there is a clear expectation that all members of a system participate in its work (Porter-O'Grady & Parker, 1997).

4. *Interdependence* - Generating shared knowledge becomes the energy force of the organization. Team members examine data to find answers and pose new questions. Together they reflect, discuss, analyze, plan and act (Lambert, 2002). Social support is the extent to which team members actively provide emotional and psychological strength to one another. This may occur through overt acts of encouragement or expressed recognition of other team members' contributions and accomplishments (Carson, 2007). Mutual recognition of the unique contribution of each individual (Jackson, 2000). The processes of empowerment operate effectively throughout the system at every point where work and relationships intersect. (Porter-O'Grady & Wilson, 1995)

5. *Ownership* - Personal commitment an individual makes to the outcomes of their work and to the mission of the organization (Porter-O'Grady, Hawkins & Parker, 1997). Clearly defined objectives, input from all member, expectations from all members (Williams, 2008). Voice is the degree to which a team's members have input into how the team carries out its purpose. When team members are able to speak up and get involved (voice), the likelihood that many of them will exercise leadership increases greatly. The opportunity for voice also facilitates shared leadership by strengthening both a common sense of direction and the potential for positive interpersonal support in a team (Carson, 2007).

I also found in my research that there are three main ways researchers are trying to measure shared leadership in teams: ratings of collective leadership behavior, social network analysis and behaviorally anchored rating scales. While social network analysis (tracking ties between team members who are perceived as exerting leadership influence on the team in a spider map diagram) and behaviorally anchored rating scales (trained raters watching team behavior either on video or in person while keeping track of specific behaviors) have been used in research, by far the most popular method being used in the research is ratings of collective leadership behavior focused on team members' perceptions of leaders within the group through conversations and surveys. In this method all team members assess the leadership qualities of all other team members. This data is then reviewed and in some cases coded to get an understanding of the shared leadership layout of the organization.

Given that the two most popular measurement methods use self-reporting within teams and that the most popular method focuses on surveys and conversations, I am confident that interviewing leaders and employees within companies will add valuable evidence to the growing body of research around shared leadership. The individuals I connected with during this research are presidents and employees who have been with their companies in most cases since the beginning. They have been tracking information about their employees and sharing it publicly for years through the B Impact Assessment but their leadership styles and practices are more elusive. With the five key characteristics of Shared Vision & Values, Trust & Openness, Accountability, Interdependence and Ownership as a foundation for my interview questions, I next moved into the definitions and major dimensions of happiness at work.

Definitions of Happiness at Work

Happiness can be a fuzzy term for scientists so they often use the term "subjective well-being" to define it. The term "subjective" focuses on the fact that how people feel is important and happiness is relative to the person who is experiencing it. "In essence," writes Achor, "the best judge of how happy you are is you. To empirically study happiness, then, scientists must rely on individual self-reports. Thankfully, after years of testing and honing survey questions on millions of people around the world, researchers have developed self-report metrics that accurately and reliably measure individual happiness" (Achor, 2010). That research helps us define the dimensions of happiness at work in the next section.

The term "well-being" hints at the fact that scientists are studying more than just feeling good and positive emotions, they are also studying life satisfaction and meaning (Crabtree, 2012). "Essentially," writes Achor, " scientists define happiness as the experience of positive emotions -pleasure combined with deeper feelings of meaning and purpose. Happiness implies a positive mood in the present and a positive outlook for the future. Studies by Martin Seligman, the pioneer in positive psychology, have confirmed (though most of us know this intuitively) that people who pursue only pleasure experience only part of the benefits happiness can bring, while those who pursue all three routes lead the fullest lives" (Achor, 2010).

In this research I refer to the word happiness rather than subjective well-being not only because it's easier and more enjoyable to read, but because it is a natural umbrella term that people use to explain how they feel about their life and work in general. It includes not only motivation and satisfaction at work but also how their work fits into the overall satisfaction and meaning in their life.

Major Dimensions of Worker Happiness

There is a wide variety of research and literature on happiness at work and for this research I wanted to identify the major dimensions of worker happiness that have been studied and operationalized within companies and organizations. From my review of research articles and literature I identified eight major dimensions to happiness at work, which I will explain with more depth in the following section:

1. *Perspective* - personal outlook on life & optimism and positivity at work

2. *Balance* – stability and solid benefits package & healthy work/life balance

3. *Autonomy* - ability to direct how/when/where we work & being trusted

4. *Mastery* – ability to develop expertise & work that fits in the "stretch zone"

5. *Purpose* – work is personally meaningful & makes a difference in the world

6. *Progress* – making progress every day & clear measured goals and performance

7. *Culture* - interpersonal support & sense of belonging at work

8. *Appreciation* – positive feedback and recognition & feeling respected

1. Perspective - Sonya Lyubomirsky, author of *The How of Happiness*, found that 40 percent of the differences in happiness levels between one person and another can be explained by factors that, unlike certain life circumstances, are directly under individuals' control. "A lot of our happiness with our job is really about how we view it. It comes from us, not necessarily just the job," (Lyubomirsky, 2008). In the journey toward success Shawn Achor, author of *The Happiness Advantage*, writes "When we are happy – when our mindsets and mood are positive – we are smarter, more motivated, and thus more successful. Happiness is the center, and success revolves around it. In an analysis of more than 200 scientific studies on nearly 275,000 people, researchers consistently found that happiness leads to success in every domain of our lives" (Achor, 2013).

2. *Balance* - So how do we help people love their jobs? Simply create environments in which they can thrive writes Simon Sinek in *Leaders Eat Last*. Sinek looked to biology and anthropology for the answers and found that employees thrive when they feel trusted and have autonomy, don't fear losing their job, feel they belong, connected to the meaning in their work and trust those around them. When deciding on one position over another 168,000 employees in

the current workforce polled by Kelly said that Work-Life Balance / Personal Fulfillment (39%) was the most important consideration (Kelly, 2012). Tal Ben-Shahar in *Happier* writes, "A human being, like a business, makes profits and suffers losses. For a human being, however, the ultimate currency is not money, nor is it any external measure, such as fame, fortune, or power. The ultimate currency for a human being is happiness." Elaborating further he adds, "Psychologist Tim Kasser shows in his research that time affluence is a consistent predictor of well-being, whereas material affluence is not. Time affluence is the feeling that one has sufficient time to pursue activities that are personally meaningful, to reflect, to engage in leisure. Time poverty is the feeling that one is constantly stressed, rushed, overworked, behind. All we need to do is look around us—and often within ourselves—to realize the pervasiveness of time poverty in our culture" (Ben-Shahar, 2007).

3. *Autonomy* - Psychologist Tim Kisser's research shows that having time affluence is a strong predictor of wellbeing, whereas material affluence is not. Time affluence allows people to personally pursue meaningful activities, to reflect more often and balance leisure with work (Ben-Shahar, 2012). Remote work can also be part of this, as Jason Fried writes in his book *Remote*, "The practice of working remotely - or telecommuting, as it's often referred to - has been silently on the rise for years. From 2005 to 2011 remote work soared 73 percent in the United States—to 3 million workers total." He quotes Sir Richard Branson on remote work as well, "To successfully work with other people, you have to trust each other. A big part of this is trusting people to get their work done wherever they are, without supervision." Either learn to trust the people you're working with or find some other people to work with" (Fried & Heinemeier, 2013).

"Autonomy, is different from independence. It's not the rugged, go-it-alone, rely-on-nobody individualism of the American cowboy," writes Dan Pink in *Drive.* Autonomy in Results Only Work Environments (ROWE) allow people to have schedules as they wish. They show up when they want, they don't have to be in the office at certain time, or anytime. They just have to get their work done. How they do it, when they do it, and where they do it is totally up to them. What happens? Almost across the board productivity goes up, worker engagement goes up, worker satisfaction goes up and turnover goes down (Pink, 2011). Amabile & Kramer also, in The Progress Principle, identified Allowing Autonomy to be one of the 7 Major Catalysts for creating an ideal work environment for progress (2011).

4. *Mastery* - In a recent survey by Kelly Services, with over 168,000 respondents in the current workforce, 74% say the key way that they derive meaning from their work is in having the 'ability to excel or develop' in their field (Kelly, 2012). Ideal workplaces, according to Dan Pink in *Drive*, "provide employees with what I call "Goldilocks tasks" – challenges that are not too hot or too cold, neither overly difficult nor overly simple." If a task is too below our capabilities, we get bored. If it's too far beyond us, we get stressed. Flow comes from engaging in tasks that stretch us just that little bit, so that we are totally engrossed in the process of attainment. The reward is in the accomplishment and sense of satisfaction that comes with it (Pink, 2008). Tal Ben-Shahar described the same thing, where the happiest people, "take risks and find their stretch zone (the healthy median between their comfort and panic zones)" (Ben-Shahar, 2007).

In his book *Flow*, Mihaly Csikszentmihalyi shares the same results, "In all the activities people in our study reported engaging in, enjoyment comes at a very specific point: whenever the opportunities for action perceived by the individual are equal to his or her capabilities. Playing tennis, for instance, is not enjoyable if the two opponents are mismatched. The less skilled player will feel anxious, and the better player will feel bored. The same is true for every other activity... Enjoyment appears at the boundary between boredom and anxiety, when the challenges are just balanced with the person's capacity to act" (Csikszentmihalyi, 1990).

5. *Purpose* - The Kelly survey also found that significant proportions of people in the workforce said issues such as their 'alignment with personal values', and 'community involvement', and 'finding meaning in their work' were central drivers of their motivation at work (Kelly, 2012). Sonya Lyubomirsky in The How of Happiness wrote, "What's interesting is that people in all kinds of jobs can see them as a calling. So it's not just for artists and neurosurgeons." (Lyubomirsky, 2008). Another greate quote comes from Tal Ben-Shahar in *Happier*, "The psychologist Abraham Maslow once wrote that 'the most beautiful fate, the most wonderful good fortune that can happen to any human being, is to be paid for doing that which he passionately loves to do'" (Ben-Shahar, 2007).

6. *Progress* - Psychologists Teresa Amabile and Steven Kramer, authors of *The Progress Principle*, interviewed over 700 managers and found 95 percent of managers misunderstood what motivates employees. After analyzing over 12,000 employee diary entries, they discovered that the number one work motivator was emotion, not financial incentive: it's the feeling of making progress every day toward a meaningful goal. "[O]ur research is unambiguous. As inner work life rises and falls, so does performance…making progress in meaningful work is the most powerful stimulant to great inner work life"(Amabile & Kramer, 2011).

7. *Culture* - Simon Sinek, in *Leaders Eat Last,* writes about companies who put a focus on building their people instead of firing them. It turns out that even if offered bigger titles and salaries, people would rather work at a place where they feel they belong, have the opportunity to

grow and feel a part of something bigger than themselves (Sinek, 2012). Authors and Gallup

Organization executives Marcus Buckingham and Curt Coffman surveyed 80,000 managers in

over 400 companies and discovered a truism: "employees join companies, but they leave their

managers." The Gallup poll found that the single most important variable in employee

productivity and loyalty is not the pay, perks, benefits. It's the quality of the relationship between

employees and their direct supervisors" (Buckingham & Coffman, 1999).

     8. Appreciation - The Progress Principle identified Major Catalysts for creating an ideal

work environment for progress, several of which revolved around communication and feedback:

Setting clear goals (knowing where you're going, and why), learning from problems and

successes (shining a non-judgmental light on failure in order to learn from it contributes to

psychological safety) and allowing ideas to flow (good communication without negativity)

(Amabile & Kramer, 2011). In the One Minute Manager, Ken Blanchard writes, "Most managers

wait until their people do something exactly right before they praise them. As a result, many

people never get to become high performers because their managers concentrate on catching

them doing things wrong – that is, anything that falls short of the final desired performance"

(Blanchard & Johnson 2007). A regular practice of reflection helps employees recognize

patterns, gain insight about your work and work relationships, celebrate and appreciate

achievements and gestures, and puzzle out what helps and hinders progress (Chen, 2012).

Amabile & Kramer, again The Progress Principle, also wrote of 4 Major Nourishers which create

an optimal environment at work, all of which fit in this dimension of happiness: Respect

(recognition, honesty, civility), encouragement (enthusiasm, expressions of confidence),

emotional support (people feel more connected when their emotions are validated by empathy)

and affiliation (actions which develop trust, appreciation, and affection) (2011).

INQUIRY DESIGN

In this section the choice of methodology, setting, data collection process, and limitations of research will be discussed in detail.

Choice of Methodology

This research focused was conducted with phenomenology in mind, where the researcher seeks to understand the meaning of individuals' experiences and how they articulate these experiences. Central to this research is the idea of caring, where the researcher inquires about the essence of lived experiences. In this kind of research a researcher looks for the essential essence of the experience where experiences contain both the outward appearance and inward consciousness based on memory, image and meaning (Williams, 2004). Further, in *Phenomenology and Psychological Research,* Amedeo Giorgo describes phenomenology as to "describe as concretely as you can a situation in which you have learned" (p. 252). In Phenomenological studies, researchers rely on interviews primarily. I conducted eight interviews with selected employees from two Certified B Corporations: SunCommon and New Media Group. These eight employees represented the full spectrum of leadership and staff positions from the traditional executive roles of Presidents to staff on the ground. Their general profiles and my rationale for choosing them as my interviewees are as follows:

1. *Mende,* Founder and President of New Media Group. Mende is the key person in setting the organization's mission and strategic vision. His opinions helped me understand the organization from the perspective of top management.

2. *Oyun*, VP of Partnerships at New Media Group, former Sales Manager. Oyun started with the company four years ago as a part-time saleswoman. Her opinions helped me understand the organization from the perspective of middle management.

3. *Zack*, Technology Team and Project Manager at New Media Group. Zack has also been with the company since the beginning. His opinions helped me understand the organization from the employee level.

4. *Ben*, Brand Manager at New Media Group. Ben works with the web development team within the company. His opinions helped me understand the organization from the employee level.

5. *Duane*, Co-Founder and Co-President of SunCommon. Duane is the key person in setting the organization's mission and strategic vision. His opinions helped me understand the organization from the perspective of top management.

6. *Carrie*, Strategy, Operations, and Sustainability at SunCommon. Carrie has helped since the beginning leading operations for the entire company. Her opinions helped me understand the organization from the perspective of top management.

7. *Jess*, Solar Organizing Manager. Jess is in charge of the entire Solar Organizers team, which are the field staff who travel throughout the state to educate and set up solar installations on residential properties. She represented middle management.

8. *Kris*, Solar Organizer. Kris is in the field working with Solar Organizers everyday. Her opinions helped me understand the organization from the employee level.

Each interviewee was asked the same questions, both "perceived" leaders within the organizations as well as staff on the ground, to determine whether the idea of leadership is pervasive throughout the company culture or not. In organizations demonstrating shared

leadership it is highly likely that staff in nontraditional leadership roles may consider themselves

leaders in the organization as much as staff in traditional leadership roles. After hours spent

reviewing the details of the B Impact assessment, I improved my interview questions

considerably and also refined my conclusions and practical applicability of this research as it

applies to future improvements to the B Impact Assessment.

The questions highlighted the five characteristics of shared leadership (*Shared Vision &*

Values, Trust & Openness, Accountability, Interdependence, Ownership) and the eight

dimensions of happiness at work (*Perspective, Balance, Autonomy, Mastery, Purpose, Progress,*

Culture, Appreciation) described above:

- Please describe your position and history with your company. (*Ownership*)

- What leadership roles have you played within your company? (*Interdependence/Autonomy*)

- What influence does leadership play in your daily work? (*Purpose/Accountability*)

- How would you describe your own leadership style? (*Leadership/Perspective/Trust*)

- How would you describe your management's communication style? (*Culture/Autonomy*)

- What are some characteristics of your company's culture? (*Values/Culture/Appreciation*)

- What influence does leadership have on that culture? (*Vision/Trust/Culture*)

- How important is personal outlook in your workplace, are things like optimism, motivation

  and happiness discussed at work? (*Perspective/Purpose/Vision/Values*)

- What benefits do you think staff enjoy most? (*Balance/Interdependence/Values*)

- Can you talk about work/life balance in your organization? (*Balance/Trust/Values/Mastery*)

- What kind of flexibility does your staff have over when, where and how they get their work

  done? (*Autonomy/Trust/Openness*)

- How does your company do professional development with staff? (*Mastery/Accountability*)

- What would be an ideal feedback system for your company? (*Mastery/Trust/Openness*)

- Would you describe your work as a calling or aligning with your personal values? How many employees do you think feel that way? (*Purpose/Progress*)

- How do employees measure their progress toward meaningful goals? (*Mastery/Progress*)

- What are some of your company's practices around reflection, appreciation, recognition and feedback? (*Appreciation/Accountability/Trust/Openness*)

- Is there anything else you would like to tell me about your company that we might have forgotten to mention? (*Perspective/Ownership*)

Though this research relies heavily on interviews, I also explored documents such as survey results from Vermont's Best Places to Work, B Corps Assessment documents and have spent time in the offices of both companies outside of the research window to gain a better understand of both organizations.

Setting of Research

The setting of inquiry was two-fold: SunCommon, a startup Certified B Corporation in its third year of operation located in Waterbury, Vermont and New Media Group, a startup Certified B Corporation in its fourth year of operation located in Ulaanbaatar, Mongolia. This research was conducted during the months of April and May 2013 and spanned over a period of six weeks. These two companies were chosen as a case study of Certified B Corporation leaders and employees to better understand how shared leadership characteristics influence worker happiness because of previous positive interactions with both organizations and recommendations from both colleagues and partners who suggested that unique practices were occurring in both organizations. Qualitative interviews were chosen as the research method to provide the most personal lens to compliment the already publicly available Certified Benefit Corporation assessments that can be found online.

Data Collection Process

First, a general meeting was held with a representative from both companies to introduce and explore details of this research project. This was done via individual phone calls and Skype meetings. This meeting explained the research and asked the participating companies if it would be acceptable to reach out to their staff for the necessary interviews. This was also an opportunity to gather supplemental data through previously administered satisfaction surveys and other measurements of employee happiness.

Second, previous surveys given to employees and assessments such as the public B Impact Assessment were explored and interview questions were developed accordingly to capture the broadest base of knowledge from the participants in the research. (See Appendix A for Interview Questions and Appendix B for B Impact Assessment).

Eight interviews were conducted and were voluntary in nature. All interviewees were over the age of 18 and were not chosen based on gender. During the interviews, participants were briefed of the voluntary nature of the process and other additional project information, such as purpose of study. The interviews were conducted over the phone or via Skype and each interview required approximately 30 minutes to complete. The interview was composed of mostly open-ended questions to allow for a more semi-structured atmosphere and elaborations upon answers.. Participants were provided with the interview questions prior to actual interview time. The interview questions were divided into sections to make sure that all characteristics of shared leadership and dimensions of happiness at work were covered; however the actual interview questionnaire given to participants did not include section titles. This was to avoid leading the interviewee to provide a certain type of answer. For instance, "Shared Leadership" as a section title on the questionnaire may have encouraged answers that included whatever the interviewee may have thought we were looking to hear.

No invasive questions were asked, and interviewees were able to decline to answer any question. There was also no direct benefit to participants for participating in this study. The general information regarding employee happiness in these companies is already public knowledge through the publicly available assessments that each company completes every year, and these interviews add a personal voice to the numbers that are already being observed. These interviews were also supplemented with that data collected through relevant Certified B Corporation documents like the B Corps Impact Assessment and company survey methods such as employee satisfaction surveys and annual happiness surveys as available (B Impact Assessment, 2014). After conducting all of the interviews, the data was organized and transcribed for easy analysis. Once this was complete, the data was interpreted to find meaning and draw conclusions for the study.

Limitations of Research

First, one limitation of this research is a small sample size. There are currently over 1,000 Certified B Corporations in the world. Speaking with two companies is a small sample size in comparison to the overall movement but given the extensive information that can be found through the B Corps Assessments that every Certified B Corporation has to publish online, these individual interviews will add a valuable personal voice to the numbers found in those lengthy assessments. In-depth interviews reveal great information but require a lot of time and attention.

Second, interviews were not conducted in person. Although phone conversations are a convenient way to gather information, it would be ideal to meet in person and video-record responses. This would allow the researcher to pick up on subtle signals from the participant.

Third, I didn't speak with everyone at the company. To gain a complete picture of a company's culture and leadership styles it would be worthwhile to spend time talking to everyone in the company. It might even be advisable to speak with employees who are no longer with the company to understand why they left. This would obviously take a lot of time, like the first limitation as well.

Fourth, the validity of the questionnaire items was being tested as I asked the questions of the interviewees. I attempted to represent the best of all the surveys and assessments I researched and include important elements from the research literature reviewed in each question but also added a final question to the interview, "Is there anything else you would like to tell me about your company that we might have forgotten to mention, especially as it relates to leadership and happiness in the workplace?" as a test of the validity of the questionnaire. As interviews progressed the questions seemed valid, clear and allowed me to clearly identify the key areas being tested throughout the interviews.

Lastly, English was the not the first language of our interviewees in the case of New Media Group. Their first language is Mongolian and, as a speaker of three languages myself, I can say with certainty that speaking in your native tongue is far easier than your second or third language. Often during our interviews it was important for me to give plenty of time for silence and reflection while team members of the New Media Group answered interview questions. To provide even more detailed answers in future studies it would be valuable to allow team members to speak in whatever language they preferred and translate the information later.

PRESENTATION AND ANALYSIS OF DATA

This section presents the results of the data collected during this research study in the form of a table, which provides an overview of all interviews, and more detailed verbal responses and segments of interviews. These responses are organized into two sections focusing on shared leadership and happiness at work subdivided into the 5 key characteristics of shared leadership and the 8 major dimensions of happiness at work. Each subdivision will clearly state how many of the eight interviews mentioned the characteristic or dimension being researched and specific examples of clearly observable activities and leadership behaviors to explain those answers when available.

Interview Data: Analysis of Data Derived from Interviews

Table 1: The following table demonstrates to what extent each key area of shared leadership and happiness at work was mentioned positively by each of the interviewees over the course of the interview. Each checkmark signifies that the particular key indicator was mentioned and validated by an interviewee in one or more questions relating to that key area. I have also divided the 8 major dimensions of happiness at work into two sub-dimensions for easier analysis.

Key Indicator	Mende	Oyun	Zack	Ben	Duane	Carrie	Jess	Kris
Characteristics of Shared Leadership								
Shared Vision & Values	✓	✓	✓	✓	✓	✓	✓	✓
Trust & Openness	✓	✓	✓	✓	✓	✓	✓	✓
Accountability	✓	✓	✓	✓	✓	✓	✓	✓
Interdependence	✓	✓	✓	✓	✓	✓	✓	✓
Ownership	✓	✓	✓		✓	✓	✓	✓

Key Indicator	Mende	Oyun	Zack	Ben	Duane	Carrie	Jess	Kris
Dimensions of Happiness at Work								
Perspective – Personal Outlook on Life	✓	✓	✓	✓	✓	✓	✓	✓
Perspective – Optimism and Positivity at Work	✓	✓	✓	✓	✓	✓	✓	✓
Balance – Stability and Solid Benefits Package	✓	✓	✓	✓	✓	✓	✓	✓
Balance – Healthy Work/Life Balance	✓	✓	✓	✓	✓	✓	✓	✓
Autonomy – Ability to Direct How You Work	✓	✓	✓	✓	✓	✓	✓	✓
Autonomy – Feeling Trusted	✓	✓	✓	✓	✓	✓	✓	✓
Mastery – Ability to Develop Expertise	✓		✓	✓	✓		✓	✓
Mastery – Work That Fits Your Stretch Zone	✓	✓	✓	✓	✓	✓	✓	✓
Purpose – Personally Meaningful Work	✓	✓	✓	✓	✓	✓	✓	✓
Purpose – Feeling You Make a Difference	✓	✓	✓	✓	✓	✓	✓	✓
Progress – Making Progress Every Day	✓	✓	✓	✓	✓	✓	✓	✓
Progress – Clear Measured Performance		✓	✓	✓	✓		✓	✓
Culture – Interpersonal Support	✓	✓	✓	✓	✓	✓	✓	✓
Culture – Sense of Belonging at Work	✓	✓	✓	✓	✓	✓	✓	✓
Appreciation – Feedback	✓	✓	✓	✓	✓	✓	✓	✓
Appreciation – Feeling Respected	✓	✓	✓	✓	✓	✓	✓	✓

Interview Data: Research Question Data Relating to Shared Leadership

Shared Vision & Values - All interviewees mentioned this area as a key focus of their everyday business. In SunCommon the all-company meetings were mentioned during every interview. "All-company meetings happen every Monday and include the entire senior leadership team updating everyone company on major indicators like sales, objectives, and new installations," Carrie said during our interview. Following this meeting individual teams meet and often one-on-one mentoring and progress updates follow that. Carrie, Kris and Jess all were very clear that Duane and the other Co-President James really set the tone for the entire organization. It was also clear through talking to Duane that he feels very passionate about the work they're doing. Many of the current employees at SunCommon, including the interviewees, first came to the organization after working with VPRG, a Vermont renewable energy advocacy organization where Duane was Chair of the Board of Trustees. As Jess said during her interview, "We all, all of us in the company, feel a clear dedication to clean energy. It's personally important to each of us and that shows up in our work." The same dedication was also seen at the New Media Group, though in a different form. New Media creates websites, marketing and software, however underlying all of that, as Oyun said, "New Media Group is a human-centered business. We care about the people in our company first, making sure that everyone is happy and doing work they love, and we also make great things for our customers." Mende sets the tone of the organization, like Duane, by having regular company meetings and offsite retreats which all interviewees at New Media Group mentioned. They are an opportunity, as Mende said, "To get to know one another better, connect personally, and also build our team together." Oyun mentioned in the beginning of her interview that she's been surprised at how many roles she has played in the company, "I started part-time in sales, then was sales manager, then viral marketing specialist, then head of the communications department and now VP of Partnerships. I guess you could say I'm a veteran in the company, I've been with it since the beginning [4 years ago]. I've always done what the company needed me to do, to be part of the team."

Trust & Openness - Trust came up during every single interview, well before I would even mention the word. It was clear that everyone not only felt connected with the vision and values at the heart of their companies, but also felt very trusted by the leadership. "When we start our company meetings," Jess said, "We always check in personally with everyone to see how they are doing. That allows us to connect to each other at a deep level. It's not just about business; it's about who we are." Also at SunCommon Carrie talked about how they have been figuring things out since the beginning, "Open communication is a hallmark of Duane and James and the way they run the team. They are always positive, clear, direct and respectful in their communication style. If someone has an idea, they want to hear it. That's also how we situated the office, with Duane and James available to everyone in the very center of our open space. There are no corner offices." I had a chance to visit the office and it was unlike any I've been in before. Everyone has a personal space, but the entire office is open. Some employees have standing desks (which I will mention later in Perspective) and others have traditional desks, but the office is organized like a large circle with the Co-Presidents and other senior staff in the center so that everyone "naturally bumps into one another and communication stays natural and open," as Duane told me when I visited the office. The word honest came up a lot in interviews as well where both the leaders and the employees feel comfortable being honest with one another not only about things happening in the company but also things happening in their personal lives. At SunCommon many of the field workers, solar organizers like Kris, work out of the office the majority of the week. They're on the road, attending meetings, organizing events, going to festivals and the company trust them to work in the interest of the organization. Kris mentioned that that "level of freedom is very empowering and shows how much the organization trusts us." New Media Group takes this trust very seriously as well, in fact it lets all of its employees choose when, how, and where they want to work. Inspired by *Getting Real* by Jason Fried, founder of Basecamp and 37signals, according to Mende his company implemented a, "Results Only Work Environment (ROWE) where basically, you are judged by the work you do in our company, not the hours you sit at a desk. Our office is open at all times for employees but no one has to come." Interestingly, their office is busy from 6am to midnight most days, with 5 to 25 employees in the office at any given time. People come in and out as they please and other employees work from, "cafes, bookstores, libraries, downtown or from home if I like," as Oyun said. "I love it," she added, "I've never worked for a company like this before."

Accountability - In the New Media Group, because of this unique ROWE strategy, accountability becomes a key issue. A lot of online tools are used for task management, such as Basecamp and Trello, but ultimately accountability comes down to the kind of relationship that each employee has with the company. As Mende said, "When we hire someone we make it clear that this is a partnership. People don't work for us, they work with us. This means that the people in our company love what they do and feel personally invested in the other people in our team." Interestingly, at SunCommon, Carrie realized during our interview that it falls within the purview of her job to improve the accountability and feedback systems within the company. As a young company they don't have the expansive 360-degree feedback systems that they would like, beyond the weekly meetings and regular individual team meetings, and that's something that Carrie said she would like to focus more time on developing herself. One that thing came up in my interview with Oyun that was very telling, and also relates to Ownership, involved her current role, "The project I am leading right now, Mende told me to treat as my own company. The final decisions about what need to be done in Mazaalai, which is a career building HR platform online, rest with me. He encouraged me to think about it as my own company within the company, and that's what I do. I feel very empowered in making decisions."

Interdependence - Creative work is at the heart of not only Mazaalai, but all of the projects that New Media Group manages. Zack and Ben talked about how important it is for the creative teams across the company to be able to work together. "We have a lot of cross-collaboration between the technology teams and creative design teams at New Media Group," said Zack, "We have to communicate with each other, whether we are programmers, designers, developers or customer-focused team members." Ben added, "As design websites for clients we have to bring a lot of people together. Nobody can do that work alone. Usually there are three to four people at least and they all have to work together understanding what the customer wants, what is possible within our systems and how to use their feedback to improve what we have created for them." In SunCommon, it's the Organizers like Kris who are on the ground with customers every day. Jess was in Kris's exact position less than a year ago and two years ago was just starting out like a lot of the members of Kris's team. "What I bring to the role of Organizer Manager," Kris told me, "is trying to make their jobs easier. I provide mentoring, share skills and tools and make sure that our Organizers have everything they need. All of us are important and essential in this process, we have to work together and find people we not only work well with, but people we genuinely like being around."

Ownership - All of the elements we mentioned before, like the weekly meetings and quarterly and yearly offsite opportunities to come together as a team allow unique opportunities for all members to share their input and expectations, success and challenges. Everyone I spoke with felt like their voice mattered, that there were regular opportunities to share their opinions and new ideas, and even run with their own projects or parts of the company - in Oyun's case that meant running her own department and later a company within the company. At SunCommon this included Carrie realizing it was within her power and a strong interest of hers to expand tools and opportunities to her team through better feedback systems. One of my favorite lines comes from Mende who said, "It's not really important who works for who. I tell my team all the time. Today I may be your boss, tomorrow your colleague and the day after I might work for you. I encourage that. I want new ideas to grow and take our company in new directions." At SunCommon I enjoyed hearing Jess talk about her leadership strategy and sharing ownership with her staff, "I guess I manage people the way I hope to be managed myself. I have sort of a high responsibility, high flexibility kind of model. There's my team and the SunCommon team, everyone is here for the same reasons, and so we kind of all start from the same motivation that we all really care about people. We all care about community and we all care about clean energy a lot. It's all about putting those pieces together and matching Organizers and their excitement around community challenges with this kind of driving force of way more solar. So recognizing that my team shares that motivation, that my job is to provide the tools and the model and the structure such that each organizer can take ownership over the work that they're doing."

Interview Data: Research Question Data Relating to Happiness at Work

Perspective - The word fun came up a lot in the interviews. Duane even has on his LinkedIn profile and other places, describing his work at SunCommon, "This is fun stuff." In Carrie's interview she said, "We are constantly doing fun events, silly things, dressing up and just enjoying being together. We try to have fun in all our communication and spend time together doing things like ride along visits where we go on sales calls with our Solar Advisors and Solar Organizers to see how things are going with installations." I also noticed that lots of employees at SunCommon have standing desks which appear handmade. "They *are* handmade," Duane told me, "From the beginning if one of our team members wanted a standing desk we would have someone come in, take measurements to find the right height based on the person and then build a desk right into the dividing wall. It's a healthy choice and we encourage that." The more I looked into it, there is a lot of research out there showing that sitting is very dangerous for our health. In fact, in one 14 year study by the American Cancer Society which tracked 123,000 Americans between 1992 and 2006, the death rates for men and women increased by 20 to 40% respectively when they sat for than six hours a day (Michaelson, 2014). From what the employees at SunCommon said, they appreciate that kind of awareness, perspective and support from their company. Similarly at New Media Group, one of the first things you see when you walk into the company is a water cooler and a pull-up bar mounted in the ceiling of the hallway. Throughout the day employees jump up on the bar, do a few pull ups and go back to their work. Zack laughed when I mentioned it, "We like to challenge each other to do more. It's fun." Healthy and happiness aren't just encouraged, they are expected at both companies. There is a walking trail around SunCommon that several interviewees mentioned loving, employees at New Media Group play soccer and basketball together on company teams outside of work and, as Jess at SunCommon said, "I couldn't imagine not having these kinds of benefits."

Balance - As Jess said so well, her job is to help her team thrive. That's at the heart of security in the workplace. "I love that, at SunCommon, they take care of things like our healthcare and sick days so we don't have to worry about that. We can just come to work and do what we love. Nobody should have to worry about those things. SunCommon pays for our healthcare, all of it, and if we need time off we get it. It's simple," said Jess. Similarly, at New Media Group, Oyun said, "At work we don't talk about work/life balance, I guess because it's just something we all have. During the four years I've been with New Media I have never heard anyone complain about not having a work life balance at all. I think the balance is perfect for people. Because we have the certain result only work environment within the company, I guess that's why a lot of the people have learned to balance their work with their personal lives and family and everything else. Being able to work flexible hours whenever we want from wherever we'd like is another really, really big advantage, something that a lot of current employees enjoy the most, including myself. I couldn't imagine not working like this."

Autonomy - Both companies give their employees a lot of autonomy, with New Media Group's results only work environment and SunCommon's employees working across the state, the idea of telecommuting was so common that it was easily forgotten by the interviewees. For Mende it isn't so much a policy as a perspective, "It's about respect and trust," he said. "We trust our team to do the work that needs to get done and we respect each other. That's how we work."

People having schedules as they wish and showing up when they want might sound too good to be true, but in these two companies it isn't. As Dan Pink wrote in Drive, when remote work becomes an option, "Almost across the board productivity goes up, worker engagement goes up, worker satisfaction goes up and turnover goes down." That's what everyone I spoke with at both New Media Group and SunCommon said as well.

Mastery - Oyun's rise from part-time salesperson to VP of Partnerships in 4 years is one of the best examples, but Jess's movement from Organizer to Lead Organizer to Organizing Manager is another great example of upward mobility in both organizations. Everyone seemed very happy in their balance between work that keeps them inspired and being part of something meaningful, without working too hard or going into the zone of getting too stressed. A challenging example however, like many social entrepreneurs, was Mende. Because he had started this company, it is also very stressful for him at times. When you are the President of an organization, it can seem hard to know how to excel or develop. You are already at the top. One of the things that Mende said he did was, "Always learn. And read. Try to expand what I know and grow and learn new things." His bookshelf is full of books like Drive, Conscious Capitalism, the 7 Habits of Highly Effective People and How to Win Friends and Influence People in both Mongolian and English. It's obvious that both companies focus a lot of attention on helping their teams optimize and play in their zones of genius, and that's something the managers have to be mindful to do for themselves as well.

Purpose - Several people used the word "calling" to describe the work that they were doing. Many of the staff at SunCommon come from advocacy backgrounds and nonprofit work, so they said they felt compelled by issues like clean energy and helping people save money and help the environment. As Jess said, "I feel lucky to do this work every day." Kris elaborated on the same point, "In my position, I sell solar. That is one of my jobs is to sell the system and I am not a salesperson. I've never been a salesperson before in my life and I certainly would not sell something I didn't 100% believe in. I wouldn't do something I wasn't proud of and this is definitely something I'm proud of every day, so it's pretty great. I think a lot of people in the company feel the same way. A lot of us have a green sense and we feel like what we're doing is the right thing to do for this planet and to have the opportunity to do it is pretty special. To be able to do it with a company that's as great as Sun Common is, it's pretty cool." At New Media Group the team regularly donates its time to nonprofits and organizations who need website development, marketing and technology support. They have also spent time organizing fund community events like TEDx and random hacks of kindness. Oyun also shared this point, "At New Media it's obvious that employees come first and we do work that we love. We try to build products that we know make a difference." Reading further in the B Corps literature I also found that "B Corps are 30% more likely than other businesses to contribute to their communities through volunteerism" (B Corps, 2014). Zack shared his feelings, "My approach to being a designer in society is that things you do should have a really big impact. And for me, it's not really worth it unless that's the case. The reason I work with NMG is because the company, as well as majority of the employees, shared similar visions and values as mine."

Progress - The importance of weekly meetings and regular team check ins can't be overstated. It's something that came up again and again in interviews with SunCommon and seems to be essential to how their team stays connected and in tune with how everyone is feeling.

Both individually and as a team it seems that this is the opportunity where everyone measures progress and knows what the next line of objectives are. Annual reviews are currently the other way people individual measure their progress. Although, as Carrie mentioned, they would like to make the process more personal and more frequent than annual. An interesting touch at New Media Group was that one of their senior staff, the VP of Knowledge, focuses his efforts on both talent retention and staff development by meeting quarterly with employees to discuss how they are feeling about the work they do and how passionate they are about their work. They try to make adjustments when needed and possible to put people into projects and assignments that best utilize their skill set and passions. Oyun added, "The great thing about the company is the fact that there aren't any limits. They don't put you inside a box and tell you stay there. If the management sees a certain employee who is having some problems, they like to talk it out, find out what is happening, what the employee is thinking, what's not working. They try to solve these problems and make sure that the team is actually satisfied with their current responsibilities and current job. That's a really big, big advantage in working with this company. Let's say I'm working as a project manager, and I don't really feel like the project I'm working on is of true value to me or the community or the country. I could go up to Mende any time, talk about it, and express my opinions and ideas. Maybe at that point Mende would ask me what I think is the best approach to making this product useful or valuable. There are a lot of interactions and communications within the company and between the team and the managers. That is I think one of the biggest advantages here. From what I see, I would pretty much say at least more than 80 percent of the current employees are pretty much where they are supposed to be and doing what they are really wanting to do. That's how I see it."

  Culture - Carrie mentioned during her interview that SunCommon was just named one of the Best Places to Work in Vermont in 2014 by the Vermont Chamber of Commerce, Vermont Department of Labor and Vermont Business Magazine (Vermont Business, 2014). In fact it was ranked #12 out of all small-to-medium sized businesses in Vermont. Even though the business has only been in operation for 2 years, it is already alongside longstanding companies like Seventh Generation (#3), VPR (#5) and AllEarth Renewables (#14) based on its score after completing the survey. Although the results of the survey are not publicly available, the full survey can be found in Appendix C. Highlights from the survey provided by the Chamber of Commerce for why SunCommon was ranked #12 in the state include: "SunCommon is committed to the triple bottom line of people, planet and profit. They are one of Vermont's pioneering Benefit Corporations and recognized as a Certified B Corporation. Most of their 65 workers operate out of The Energy Mill, New England's largest net-zero office building. Field staff are provided hybrid vehicles, honored with solid benefits, open-book financials are shared, and there are frequent employee-organized parties and meals are provided during all-company meetings. At SunCommon, they aspire for their work to be both fulfilling and fun." This was highlighted in the interviews as well, Carrie, Kris and Jess all mentioned that the culture at SunCommon wasn't just apparent within the relationships between staff but also the environment within the office. The way they've designed the space, the commitment to a natural and comfortable office space, the walking trails outside, everything is built around the needs of the staff. Furthermore, as an environmental company, the staff I interviewed felt proud that their personal values like using renewable energy as much as possible, environmental advocacy, limited waste creation and having a strong and cohesive team was also matched in their physical workspace. At the New Media Group, Zack mentioned a similar sentiment, "The reason I work with NMG is because the company, as well as majority of the employees, shared similar visions and values as mine. It is very important to keep the optimism, motivation, and happiness level as high as possible so the employees can deliver the best possible results. NMG organizes monthly events, fun activities, and discussions in which majority of the employees participate." Oyun shared the same thoughts, "New Media is a very human centered company. The core of the company is the people, the team. In everything we do we like to make sure that it's not only in the favor of our customers but, more importantly, of our team as well. We like to make sure that whatever the team is working on, whatever the tasks are, we like to make sure that they're also getting some sort of satisfaction out of what they're doing." She elaborated, "I guess we have a lot of team time. We go out to play basketball or go out to the countryside for a vacation a few nights. We also organize certain events for mixing and mingling." Mende shared the same thoughts, "Every month we pick one Saturday and we gather and we play a lot of games. We solve some puzzles for teambuilding purposes. We announce best team member of the month, we do surveys and challenge ourselves. Sometimes we'll invite a family member of a team member. It gives them the opportunity to see what we're actually doing and how we could maybe improve the environment and workflow and everything. We also celebrate that month's birthdays. It's just a fun time to be there." The American Society for Quality also highlighted these activities when they named New Media Group as one of ten organizations worldwide in its Pathways to Social Responsibility alongside 3M and Microsoft. In the report ASQ writes, "NMG emphasizes the engagement of its employees and external stakeholders in its business planning and management processes. Regular community meetings across the organization help NMG monitor how the organization is doing on its social, environmental, and workplace goals. Finally, NMG's Vice President of Knowledge, provides individualized personal development plans with each employee to understand how they are developing within the NMG team and in support of NMG's mission" (ASQ, 2014).

Appreciation - All SunCommon team members mentioned that all-company meetings were a regular place for recognition and appreciation. "Duane usually calls people out who have really done an outstanding job, like he did with Dave at our last all-company meeting," Jess shared, "Dave had hit a record number of sales for that month and Duane wanted to make sure he felt appreciated. Those kinds of things happen all the time and it feels really nice." New Media also gives out yearly awards to staff and on a regular basis tries to show appreciation to their team through an annual event celebrating the anniversary of the company, TEDx events organized by the team several times a year and other conferences and large-scale events organized by the team such as the national bloggers event and others. Zack and Ben also mentioned that Mende is good at "catching people doing things right," and trying to make sure people notice when team members are doing outstanding work.

DISCUSSION

SunCommon and New Media Group represent a new trend in business, not only because they are members of the Certified B Corporation movement but because of the way they operate day to day. As Jess said in her interview, "I have never worked at a company like this in my life, and I've worked at a lot of companies." I feel the same way personally about New Media Group and I have told Mende that every time we have met since our very first meeting. In the past we left that kind of feeling to clubs and religious spaces, places where we could truly be ourselves and connect to other like-minded people. It seems that these unique businesses are creating a new place for us where the teams involved can not only do things that they find meaningful but also find personal and professional happiness.

Conclusions

The results of these interviews point to several conclusions. First, the five characteristics of shared leadership and the eight dimensions of happiness at work were validated by each of the eight interviews as being significant factors in the experiences of each interviewee. The majority of the interviewees mentioned each of them several times and a common refrain from every interviewee was that these qualities made their organizations special places to work. Statements like "I've never worked in a place like this," or "I couldn't imagine working with a company that didn't do these things," were also commonplace.

Second, there was clear collaboration between the shared leadership characteristics and the happiness at work dimensions and they were mentioned together countless times throughout the interviews. Shared Vision & Values blended into Purpose and Culture, Trust & Openness directly impacted Balance, Autonomy and Perspective, Accountability powered Progress and Mastery, Interdependence reflected Appreciation and Culture, and Ownership clearly affected Purpose. The characteristics and dimensions crisscrossed so much in fact, it was hard to pull them apart. It might even be possible to blend them together into a single set of characteristics of happy leadership. I think that merits further research and I will discuss it later.

Third, this research clearly demonstrates that there are stories worth being told that aren't currently being captured in surveys and assessments. The interviewees were very happy to share these detailed stories and were happy someone was taking the time to listen to them. These are stories of changed lives, of great companies who are making a difference in the world and setting an example that could improve communities around the world. It was clear that employees in these two companies wished more people could work for companies like theirs. I share that view.

Research Impact

It was my intention that this research build upon the great work that has been done in the field of shared leadership and attempt to fill in some of the gaps in research that have been identified by scholars. While shared leadership has been studied and demonstrated to improve team productivity, engagement, performance and empowerment, none of these studies have looked at the influence shared leadership has on employee happiness or the connection that shared leadership has to the growing Certified Benefit Corporation movement. Given the positive impact of shared leadership, I thought it would be valuable to understand if shared leadership principles are being used in successful organizations to improve worker happiness. This also falls squarely in the area where scholars have indicated more research needs to be done: the outcomes of shared leadership.

The current research provides a great foundation for definitions and qualities of shared leadership and also highlights the need for organizations to think in new ways and question the vertical approach to leadership. This research adds to the effort to bring to light the alternative forms of leadership that exist and highlight the new perspectives that make these leadership approaches possible. Furthermore much of the current literature has focused on the qualities and benefits of shared leadership without explaining how shared leadership comes about according to the leaders and organizations that make the choice to engage in it. This study highlights startup companies that are using creative new leadership models within the relatively new phenomenon of Certified Benefit Corporation movement.

By exploring the measurements already being done through publicly available Benefit Corporation assessments and matching them with in-person interviews to highlight the influence shared leadership principles are having on workplace happiness, this study adds valuable insight into this important area at a time when our communities and companies need it most. The conclusions of this research have clear implications for companies who want to increase productivity and happiness while providing an accessible way for supervisors to be better leaders.

Practical Applicability

Right now survey tools like the Best Places to Work in Vermont and the B Impact Assessment are relatively commonplace, but through in-depth conversations with these two companies and many others, it seems clear to me that many companies have a hard time measuring workplace happiness. For instance, the term "annual review" isn't conjuring up positive images for anyone, employees or management, even though that is potentially one of the greatest opportunities a company has to engage with its team and talk about what could be going better. The epiphany that Carrie said herself in our interview is one that anyone at any company could have, "What *is* an ideal feedback system for us? I hadn't really thought of that. Actually… the more I think about it, that's something I could start creating right now. I think I'm going to." In just a few minutes Carrie went from learning about improving the company, to imagining it, to taking personal responsibility for creating it. That's one of the best examples of shared leadership, employee empowerment and happiness at work I can think of. I could hear it in her voice and I look forward to staying in touch with her to see how things move forward.

Further, in the case of B Lab (the nonprofit supporting the B Corporation movement), a new version of the B Impact Assessment comes out every year improving upon previous versions. At this year's Champions Retreat, which will bring together Certified B Corporations from all over the world right here in Burlington, Vermont, I will bring my research and talk with the leadership at B Lab to see if there are ways we can expand the assessment to ask more questions around the five characteristics of shared leadership and the eight dimensions of happiness at work. I believe they would find fascinating information and wonderful stories, just like the stories in this research, if they would ask their more than 1,000 currently Certified B Corporations in over 30 countries and it would be incredible to be part of that.

Recommendations for Further Research

A more thorough study would be very valuable not only to the business community, but to the academic community as well. There are unique and, in my opinion, frankly amazing things happening in these organizations and that is a story that deserves to be told. We all want to do work that we believe in, provide for our families and be part of communities we are proud of. The current books coming out, such as the B Corps Handbook written by Ryan Honeyman that comes out in October, will continue to shine light on these stories but there is a lot left to tell.

The surveys and assessments are a great start and certainly help companies remain accountable and transparent, but continuing to do research by asking about personal experiences and stories will explain to people in real terms what kinds of differences these companies are making in the lives of people around the world. And in fact, in their own way, they are changing the world forever.

BIBLIOGRAPHY

Achor, S. (2010). *The happiness advantage: the seven principles of positive psychology that fuel success and performance at work.* New York: Broadway Books.

Alvesson, M., & Sveningsson, S. (2003). The great disappearing act: difficulties in doing 'leadership.', The Leadership Quarterly,14,359-381.

Amabile, T., & Kramer, S. (2011). *The progress principle.* New York, NY: Harvard Business Review Press.

Amartaivan, Mende. (2014, 05 5). Interview by Travis Hellstrom. New Media Group.

ASQ. (2014) American Society for Quality 2014 Pathways for Social Responsibility. Retrieved from: http://static.squarespace.com/static/51db2e33e4b0afd8bc85afce/t/5350370fe4b0d2db445382fc/1397765903175/Pathways%202014.pdf

B Impact Assessment 101. (2014). Retrieved from http://www.bcorporation.net/b-impact-assessment-101

B Corps (2014). Retrieved from http://www.bcorporation.net

Batbaatar, Ben. (2014, 05 2). Interview by Travis Hellstrom. New Media Group.

Batsaikhan, Zack. (2014, 04 27). Interview by Travis Hellstrom. New Media Group.

Ben-Shahar, T. (2007). *Happier.* New York: McGraw-Hill.

Bergman, J. Z., Rentsch, J. R., Small, E. E., Davenport, S.W., & Bergman, S. M. (2012). The shared leadership process in decision-making teams, *The Journal of Social Psychology,* 152, 1, 17-42.

Blanchard, K. H., & Johnson, S. (2007). *The one minute manager.* New York: Morrow.

Bligh, M., Pearce, C., & Kohles, J. (2006). The importance of self- and shared
leadership in team based knowledge work: a meso-level model of leadership
dynamics. *Journal of Managerial Psychology, 21(4), 296-318.*

Bolden, R. (2004). What is Leadership? Leadership South West Research Report, Centre for
Leadership Studies, July 2004.

Bolman, L.G., & Deal, T. E. (1991). Reframing organizations: artistry, choice, and leadership.
San Francisco: Jossey-Bass.

Buckingham, M., & Coffman, C. (1999). First, break all the rules: what the world's greatest
managers do differently. New York, NY.: Simon & Schuster.

Carbine-March, Carrie. (2014, 04 22). Interview by Travis Hellstrom. SunCommon.

Carson, J. B, Tesluk, P. E., & Marrone, J. A. (2007). Shared leadership in teams: An
investigation   of antecedent conditions and performance. *Academy of Management
Journal*, 50, 5, 1217-1234.

Chen, W. (2012). The science behind what motivates us to get up for work every day. Retrieved
from http://lifehacker.com/5945221/the-science-behind-what-motivates-us-to-get-up-for-
work-every-day

Covey, S. R. (2013). The 7 habits of highly effective people (25th anniversary ed.). London:
Simon & Schuster.

Crabtree, S. (2012). *This Is Your Brain on Gratitude.*

Crabtree, S. (2014, 04 12). Interview by Travis Hellstrom [Personal Interview]. Happy brain
science.

Crutchfield, L., & McLeod-Grant, H. (2012). Forces for Good: The Six Practices of High-
Impact Nonprofits. Revised and Updated. USA: John Wiley & Sons, Inc.

Csikszentmihalyi, M. (1990). Flow: the psychology of optimal experience. New York: Harper & Row.

Giorgo, Amedeo. (1985). *Phenomenology and psychological research.* Pittsburgh: Duquesne University Press.

Halverson, C. B., & Tirmizi, S. A. (2008). *Effective multicultural teams: theory and practice.* Dordrecht: Springer.

Hersey, P. and Blanchard, K. (1988). *Management of organizational behavior: Utilizing human resources* (5th Ed.). Englewood Cliffs, NJ: Prentice-Hall.

Horner, M. (1997). Leadership theory: past, present and future. *Team Performance Management*, 3(4): 270-287.

Jackson, S. (2000). A qualitative evaluation of shared leadership barriers, drivers and recommendations. *ALO Journal*, 1, 141.

Kaplan, R. S., (2001). Strategic Performance Measurement and Management in Nonprofit Organizations. Nonprofit Management & Leadership, 11(3), 353-370.

Lambert, L. (2002). A framework for shared leadership. *Beyond Instructional Leadership*, 59(8), 37-40.

Lyubomirsky, S., King, L., & Diener, E. (2005). The benefits of frequent positive affect: Does happiness lead to success? Psychological Bulletin, 131, 803–855."

Lyubomirsky, S. (2008). *The how of happiness: A scientific approach to getting the life you want.* New York: Penguin Press

Performance Requirements. (2014). Retrieved from http://www.bcorporation.net/become-a-b-corp/how-to-become-a-b-corp/performance-requirements

Peterson, Duane. (2014, 04 25). In-Person Conversation with Travis Hellstrom. B Local Meeting at SunCommon in Waterbury, VT.

Pink, D. (2011). Why progress matters: 6 questions for harvard's teresa amabile. Retrieved from http://www.danpink.com/2011/08/why-progress-matters-6-questions-for-harvards-teresa-amabile/

Porter-O'Grady, Tim, Marilyn Hawkins, and Marsha Parker. 1997. *Whole Systems Shared Governance*. Aspen Publication. Maryland p40

Ramsey, N. (2012). Happiness & meaning at work. Kelly. Retrieved from http://www.kellyocg.com/Knowledge/Whitepaper_Content Happiness_and_Meaning_at_Work_White_Paper/

Seid, E. (1997). The Role of Leadership in a Start-up Organization, in a U.S. American Context, Capstone. School for International Training.

Silverblatt, R. (2010). The science of workplace happiness. Retrieved from http://money.usnews.com/money/careers/articles/2010/04/14/the-science-of-workplace-happiness

Sinek, S. (2014). *Leaders eat last.* New York: Portfolio.

Michaelson.(2014) Sitting Vs. Standing Desk. Retrieved: http://visual.ly/sitting-vs-standing-desk

Thomas, G., Martin, R., & Riggio, R. (2013). Leading groups: Leadership as a group process. *Group Processes Intergroup Relations* (16)3.

Valade, Kris. (2014, 05 4). Interview by Travis Hellstrom. SunCommon.

Vermont Business Magazine. (2014). Vermont Business Magazine names Best Places to Work in Vermont. Retrieved from: http://www.vermontbiz.com/news/march/vermont-business-magazine-names-best-places-work-vermont

Vladimir, Oyun. (2014, 05 5). Interview by Travis Hellstrom. New Media Group.

Walsh, Jess. (2014, 05 4). Interview by Travis Hellstrom. SunCommon.

Williams. K. (2003). *Qualitative Data Collection Types, Options, Advantages, and Limitations.*

    SIT Graduate Institute.

Williams, K. (2008) Effective leadership for multicultural teams. In Halverson, C. B., & Tirmizi,

    S. A. (Eds.), *Effective multicultural teams: theory and practice.* (pp. 151-154) Dordrecht:

    Springer.

Appendix A: *Interview Consent Form & Questionnaire*

**SIT Graduate Capstone Research
Interview Consent Form**

You are invited to participate in a research project focusing on "How shared leadership influences worker happiness within Certified Benefit Corporations?" The study is being conducted by Travis Hellstrom, a graduate student from SIT Graduate Institute, which is located in Brattleboro, Vermont.

This interview is comprised of open-ended questions in a semi-structured format. It will take approximately 30 minutes to complete. The interview will be conducted by phone, Skype, Google Hangouts or face-to-face. The interview is voluntary in nature and as such you can choose to quit at any time. If you decide not to participate, there will be no negative consequences.

If you have any questions, you may contact Travis Hellstrom at (828) 330-4335. The Human Subjects Review Board has approved this consent document and interview questions.

By writing your name below, you agree to complete the survey. The survey is voluntary. Every effort to keep the information collected confidential.

Name (please print):

_____

Name (signature):

_____

Date: _____

Date of Birth: _____

Email: _____

Interview Questions:
Shared Leadership & Happiness at Work Interview

You are invited to participate in a research project focusing on "How shared leadership influences worker happiness within Certified Benefit Corporations?" The study is being conducted by Travis Hellstrom, a graduate student from SIT Graduate Institute, which is located in Brattleboro, Vermont.

This interview is comprised of open-ended questions in a semi-structured format. It will take approximately 30 minutes to complete. The interview will be conducted by phone, Skype, Google Hangouts or face-to-face. The interview is voluntary in nature and as such you can choose to quit at any time. If you decide not to participate, there will be no negative consequences. If you have any questions, you may contact Travis Hellstrom at (828) 330-4335. The Human Subjects Review Board has approved this consent document and interview questions.

Today's Date: _____

- **Intro/Leadership** - Please describe your position and history with your company.
- **Leadership/Autonomy** - What leadership roles have you played within your company?
- **Leadership/Purpose** - What influence does leadership play in your daily work?
- **Leadership/Perspective** - How would you describe your own leadership style?
- **Culture/Autonomy** - How would you describe your management's communication style?
- **Culture/Appreciation** - What are some characteristics of your company's culture?
- **Leadership/Culture** - What influence does leadership have on that culture?
- **Perspective/Purpose** - How important is personal outlook in your workplace, are things like optimism, motivation and happiness discussed at work?
- **Balance** – What are some of the benefits that you think your staff enjoy the most?
- **Balance** - Can you talk about work/life balance in your organization?
- **Autonomy** - What kind of flexibility does your staff have over when, where and how they get their work done?
- **Mastery** - How does your company encourage professional development with staff?
- **Mastery** – What do you think would be an ideal feedback system for your company?
- **Purpose/Progress** - Would you describe your work as a calling or aligning with your personal values? How many employees do you think feel that way?
- **Progress** - How do your employees measure their progress toward meaningful goals?
- **Appreciation** - What are some of your company's practices around reflection, appreciation, recognition and feedback?
- **Perspective** – Is there anything else you would like to tell me about your company that we might have forgotten to mention?

Appendix B: *B Impact Assessment Worker Happiness Questions*

The workers section of the B Impact Assessment assesses each company's relationship to its workforce through 10 areas: how the company treats its workers through compensation, benefits, training, ownership opportunities, work environment, management communication, job flexibility, corporate culture, and worker health and safety. While it wouldn't be prudent to include all of the questions in the 10 areas of the assessment, I will include several highlights which had implications for my research:

- What % above the living wage did your lowest-paid worker receive this year?
- What multiple is the highest compensated individual paid (inclusive of bonus) as compared to the lowest paid full-time worker?
- Is health insurance offered to all full-time employees and their families and what % of paid health insurance premiums for coverage do full-time workers receive?
- What % of the company is owned or formally reserved as part of a written plan for full-time workers and management excluding founders/executives?
- Is there an established, formal, consistent process for providing performance feedback to all employees which is conducted on at least an annual basis, includes peer and subordinate input, provides written guidance for career development, includes social and environmental goals and clearly identifies achievable goals?
- Does the company systematically solicit feedback on employee satisfaction / engagement on at least an annual basis?
- Are full-time employees explicitly allowed paid or non-paid time-off hours options for community service?
- Has the company created a public partnership with a service organization to which it consistently supplies both promotion and volunteer or financial support?
- What was the % of profits or revenues that your company gave to Carrie in the reporting period? Which organizations does your company support?
- Is there something different or innovative about the company's worker ownership structure that changed the industry?

Appendix C: *Best Places to Work in Vermont Survey*

Best Companies Group ▶▶▶

Employee Engagement and Satisfaction Survey

Fill in each circle completely using a DARK BLUE or BLACK PEN, not a pencil. Do not use "x" or "/" marks. To ensure your anonymity, mail your completed survey in the postage-paid envelope provided. Upon receipt of your survey, your answers and comments will be added to those of your fellow workers and summarized as a group. The number in the right hand corner of this document is for data processing only and cannot be tracked to any individual's survey responses. If you have any questions or comments contact Best Companies Group at support@bestcompaniesgroup.com.

	Disagree Strongly	Disagree Somewhat	Neutral	Agree Somewhat	Agree Strongly	Not Applicable
1. Overall, I am very satisfied with my employer	O	O	O	O	O	O

How do you feel about each of the following specific matters? (Fill in a single response for each statement below)

2. This organization's leadership and planning:

	Disagree Strongly	Disagree Somewhat	Neutral	Agree Somewhat	Agree Strongly	Not Applicable
I understand the long-term strategy of this organization	O	O	O	O	O	O
I have confidence in the leadership of this organization	O	O	O	O	O	O
The leaders of this organization care about their employees' well being	O	O	O	O	O	O
Senior leaders live the core values of the organization	O	O	O	O	O	O
There is adequate planning of departmental objectives	O	O	O	O	O	O
There is adequate follow-through of departmental objectives	O	O	O	O	O	O
The leaders of this organization are open to input from employees	O	O	O	O	O	O

3. The organization's corporate culture and communications:

	Disagree Strongly	Disagree Somewhat	Neutral	Agree Somewhat	Agree Strongly	Not Applicable
This organization's corporate communications are frequent enough	O	O	O	O	O	O
This organization's corporate communications are detailed enough	O	O	O	O	O	O
I have a good understanding of how this organization is doing financially	O	O	O	O	O	O
I can trust what this organization tells me	O	O	O	O	O	O
This organization treats me like a person, not a number	O	O	O	O	O	O
This organization gives me enough recognition for work that is well done	O	O	O	O	O	O
Staffing levels are adequate to provide quality products/services	O	O	O	O	O	O
Quality is a top priority with this organization	O	O	O	O	O	O
Safety is a top priority with this organization	O	O	O	O	O	O
I believe there is a spirit of cooperation within this organization	O	O	O	O	O	O
My employer enables a culture of diversity	O	O	O	O	O	O
I like the people I work with at this organization	O	O	O	O	O	O
At this organization, employees have fun at work	O	O	O	O	O	O
I feel I can express my honest opinions without fear of negative consequences	O	O	O	O	O	O
Changes that may affect me are communicated to me prior to implementation	O	O	O	O	O	O

Appendix C con't: ***Best Places to Work in Vermont Survey***

Best Companies Group▶▶▶

Employee Engagement and Satisfaction Survey

Fill in each circle completely using a DARK BLUE or BLACK PEN, not a pencil. Do not use "x" or "/" marks. To ensure your anonymity, mail your completed survey in the postage-paid envelope provided. Upon receipt of your survey, your answers and comments will be added to those of your fellow workers and summarized as a group. The number in the right hand corner of this document is for data processing only and cannot be tracked to any individual's survey responses. If you have any questions or comments contact Best Companies Group at support@bestcompaniesgroup.com.

	Disagree Strongly	Disagree Somewhat	Neutral	Agree Somewhat	Agree Strongly	Not Applicable
1. Overall, I am very satisfied with my employer	○	○	○	○	○	○

How do you feel about each of the following specific matters? (Fill in a single response for each statement below)

2. This organization's leadership and planning:	Disagree Strongly	Disagree Somewhat	Neutral	Agree Somewhat	Agree Strongly	Not Applicable
I understand the long-term strategy of this organization	○	○	○	○	○	○
I have confidence in the leadership of this organization	○	○	○	○	○	○
The leaders of this organization care about their employees' well being	○	○	○	○	○	○
Senior leaders live the core values of the organization	○	○	○	○	○	○
There is adequate planning of departmental objectives	○	○	○	○	○	○
There is adequate follow-through of departmental objectives	○	○	○	○	○	○
The leaders of this organization are open to input from employees	○	○	○	○	○	○

3. The organization's corporate culture and communications:	Disagree Strongly	Disagree Somewhat	Neutral	Agree Somewhat	Agree Strongly	Not Applicable
This organization's corporate communications are frequent enough	○	○	○	○	○	○
This organization's corporate communications are detailed enough	○	○	○	○	○	○
I have a good understanding of how this organization is doing financially	○	○	○	○	○	○
I can trust what this organization tells me	○	○	○	○	○	○
This organization treats me like a person, not a number	○	○	○	○	○	○
This organization gives me enough recognition for work that is well done	○	○	○	○	○	○
Staffing levels are adequate to provide quality products/services	○	○	○	○	○	○
Quality is a top priority with this organization	○	○	○	○	○	○
Safety is a top priority with this organization	○	○	○	○	○	○
I believe there is a spirit of cooperation within this organization	○	○	○	○	○	○
My employer enables a culture of diversity	○	○	○	○	○	○
I like the people I work with at this organization	○	○	○	○	○	○
At this organization, employees have fun at work	○	○	○	○	○	○
I feel I can express my honest opinions without fear of negative consequences	○	○	○	○	○	○
Changes that may affect me are communicated to me prior to implementation	○	○	○	○	○	○

Appendix C con't: ***Best Places to Work in Vermont Survey***

Best Companies Group▶▶▶

8. Pay and Benefits:	Disagree Strongly	Disagree Somewhat	Neutral	Agree Somewhat	Agree Strongly	Not Applicable
My pay is fair for the work I perform	O	O	O	O	O	O
Overall, I'm satisfied with this organization's benefits package	O	O	O	O	O	O

Specifically, I'm satisfied with the:

Amount of vacation (or Paid Time Off)	O	O	O	O	O	O
Sick leave policy	O	O	O	O	O	O
Amount of health care paid for	O	O	O	O	O	O
Dental benefits	O	O	O	O	O	O
Vision care benefits	O	O	O	O	O	O
Retirement plan benefits	O	O	O	O	O	O
Life insurance benefits	O	O	O	O	O	O
Disability benefits	O	O	O	O	O	O
Tuition reimbursement benefits	O	O	O	O	O	O

9. Overall feelings about your employment experience:	Disagree Strongly	Disagree Somewhat	Neutral	Agree Somewhat	Agree Strongly	Not Applicable
Most days, I look forward to going to work	O	O	O	O	O	O
My job provides me with a sense of meaning and purpose	O	O	O	O	O	O
I am proud to work for this organization	O	O	O	O	O	O
I feel this organization has created an environment where I can do my best work	O	O	O	O	O	O
I am willing to give extra effort to help this organization succeed	O	O	O	O	O	O
I plan to continue my career with this organization for at least two more years	O	O	O	O	O	O
I would recommend this organization's products/services to a friend	O	O	O	O	O	O
I would recommend working here to a friend	O	O	O	O	O	O

> NOTE: We recommend that you do not include your name or other identifying remarks in your responses to the two open-ended questions listed below. PLEASE DO NOT EXCEED THE SPACE PROVIDED BELOW.
> **Please do not use symbols or characters such as (=,$,%,@,!,$,&,*,_,+)**

10. What does this organization do that makes it a place where people would want to work?

_____
_____
_____
_____
_____

11. What can this organization do to increase your satisfaction and productivity as an employee?

_____
_____
_____
_____
_____

Appendix C con't: ***Best Places to Work in Vermont Survey***

Best Companies Group▶▶▶

> The following questions are for classification purposes only. They will not be used to identify any individual.
> Please fill in only one response per question.

12. How long have you worked for this organization?

Less than one year .... ○
One year to less than two years.................... ○
Two years to less than five years .... ○
Five years to less than ten years.................. ○
Ten years or more .... ○
Prefer not to answer .... ○

13. What is your age?

Less than 21 .... ○
21 - 25... ○
26 - 35... ○
36 - 45... ○
46 - 55... ○
56 - 65... ○
Above 65.. ○
Prefer not to answer .... ○

14. What is your gender?

Female .... ○
Male... ○
Prefer not to answer .... ○

15. What is your ethnic background?

Black or African-American .... ○
Asian.. ○
White or Caucasian...................................... ○
Hispanic or Latino .... ○
Native American (not Pacific Islander) .... ○
Pacific Islander .... ○
Bi-Racial or Multi-Racial .... ○
Prefer not to answer .... ○

16. Which is your job status?

Full-Time.. ○
Part-Time... ○

17. Which of the following best describes your role?

Administrative/Clerical .... ○
Executive/Partner .... ○
Manager or Supervisor .... ○
Production/Service .... ○
Professional .... ○
Other.. ○

18. In which department do you work?

Customer Service/Care/Support .... ○
Development/Fundraising .... ○
Finance/Accounting...................................... ○
Human Resources... ○
Information Technology............................... ○
Legal... ○
Marketing/Advertising .... ○
Maintenance/Operations.............................. ○
Production .... ○
Research & Development.............................. ○
Sales/Retail/Business Development .... ○
Other.. ○

Thank You for Your Participation!
For questions or comments, please email support@bestcompaniesgroup.com.

Appendix D: ***B Corporation Declaration of Interdependence***

Declaration of Interdependence

We envision a new sector of the economy
which harnesses the power of private enterprise to create public benefit.
This sector is comprised of a new type of corporation — the B Corporation —
which is purpose-driven, and creates benefit for all stakeholders, not just shareholders.

As members of this emerging sector and as entrepreneurs and investors in B Corporations,

We hold these truths to be self-evident:

That we must be the change we seek in the world.

That all business ought to be conducted as if people and place mattered.

That, through their products, practices, and profits, businesses should aspire to do no harm and benefit all.

To do so, requires that we act with the understanding that we are each dependent upon another and thus responsible for each other and future generations.

the change we seek™

"Happiness is the meaning and the purpose of life, the whole aim and end of human existence." Aristotle